UNPLUGGED
HOW TO DISCONNECT AND FIND PEACE IN A NOISY WORLD

Unplugged: How to Disconnect and Find Peace in a Noisy World
Copyright © 2016, 2019 by Orlando U. Javien Jr.
All rights reserved.

No part of this publication may be reproduced, stored in a retrieval system or transmitted in any way by any means, electronic, mechanical, photocopy, recording or otherwise without the prior permission of the author except as provided by USA copyright law.

Old and New Testament revised A.D. 1881-1885 and A.D. 1901 (Apocrypha revised A.D. 1894). Compared with the most ancient authorities and revised A.D. 1952 (Apocrypha revised A.D. 1957). The original Catholic edition of the RSV translation was prepared by the Catholic Biblical Association of Great Britain.

New Testament, copyright 1946, Old Testament, copyright 1962, The Apocrypha copyright 1957. Revised Standard Version. Catholic Edition. Copyright © 1965, 1966. Division of Christian Education of the National Council of the Churches of Christ in the United States of America.

Revised Standard Version Bible, Ignatius Edition, Copyright © 2006, Division of Christian Education of the National Council of the Churches of Christ in the United States of America. Used by permission. All rights reserved.

Book interior design by Inspire Books
www.inspire-books.com
Cover Design Denise Maher
Illustrations Junior Javien and Jennilyn Javien
Photography Sharon Cooley

Printed in the United States

ISBN: 978-1-950685-16-5 paperback
ISBN: 978-1-950685-17-2 ebook
1. Biography & Autobiography/ Personal Memoirs
2. Religion/ Christian Life/ General

UNPLUGGED
HOW TO DISCONNECT AND FIND PEACE IN A NOISY WORLD

Orlando U. Javien, Jr.

DEDICATION

To my wife Beth, my son Junior, and my daughter Jennilyn. Thank you for allowing me to dream big. I love you all the time!

ACKNOWLEDGMENTS

> A faithful friend is a sturdy shelter: he that has found one has found a treasure. There is nothing so precious as a faithful friend, and no scales can measure his excellence.
>
> —Sirach 6:14–15

I have been blessed with many treasures in my life's journey. I thank you, Lord, for the mountains and the trees, the sun above my head, and for breath of life. All the glory and praise belongs to you.

To my wife, Beth, and my children Junior and Jennilyn, thank you for your illustrations and being the inspiration to my stories.

To my mom and dad, your support and guidance has allowed me to seek out the most important things in life.

To my brothers, sister, and in-laws—Kelvin and Cheryl, Yvonne and Mike, Joseph and Krystal, Johanne, Mackie, and Beth's parents, thank you for your support and encouragement.

To my nephews and nieces—Alyssa, Justin, Brianna, Kelan, Kyla and Karter, I pray that this book opens your eyes to how simple faith can be.

To my wrestling coach, Jose Campo, thank you for guidance and instilling in me godly principles.

Thank you to the Tuesday-morning prayer group that kick started my faith journey eight years ago. To the Friday-night Bible study group, St. Michael's Men's group, Cursillo of San Diego, Knights of Columbus, and the Benedictus group, thank you for sharpening me.

"As iron sharpens iron, so one man sharpens another" (Prov. 27:17).

And finally, for the many people who have crossed my path, thank you for lending me your ear.

Dream no small dreams for they have no power to move the hearts of men.
—**Johann von Goethe**

CONTENTS

Foreword by Auxiliary Bishop John Dolan xiii
Stop Googling Yourself 1
Faith Is a Verb 5
I Can Touch My Toes 9
Daddy, How Should I Pray? 13
I Can't Find Jesus! 17
Church Is Boring 21
Lord, I'll Shut Up Now! 25
Healing Begins with You! 29
The Gospel According to Friends 33
Happy Wife, Happy Life Is a Myth 37
Too Many Water Bottles 41
I Hate Ants! 43
Move the Couch Please! 47
The Gospel According to Batman 51
Discipline: Please, Sir, Can I Have Some More! 55
I Don't Want to Do the Dishes! 59
God Is Not Sending Me to Africa! 63
I'm Not Called to Save Lives 67
Come See a Man! 69
I See You! 73
You Don't Know Me! 77
How Many Saturdays Do You Have Left? 81
About the Author 85

FOREWORD

If the ability to laugh at oneself is a virtue, then Orlando Javien embraces that virtue. After reading his first book, *God Moments: Why God Made Me Pick Up Underwear and Other Stories of Faith*, I was immediately struck by the humility and wit of this deeply spiritual man. His second book follows the same thread as his first and is equally humorous and to the point. Sharing personal experiences of family, work, and physical exercise to illustrate his spiritual theology, Orlando opens our eyes to the reality that he is not perfect. He goes on to show that even in our common human imperfection, our perfect God loves us perfectly.

Building on his self-admitted imperfection, Orlando shows how a humble person may find joy—not to be confused with happiness—in seeking Christ in this imperfect world.

While recognizing that the noise of the world exists around us, we do not have to make it our own. When we make it our own, we become false masters of ourselves and become narcissistic. We start googling ourselves.

This is different than blocking the noise of family, work, and exercise out in order to live in a quiet relationship with the Lord. Rather, even in our hustle and bustle of life, we can experience the calm of the Lord everywhere, even at the movies.

While the noise continues, we seek Christ and proclaim him. Our Christian mission is not put on hold until the noise subsides. Orlando invites us to practice our relationship with Christ while the messiness of life continues around us. He advises us to step into the Word of God through Scripture, prayer, and church and relationships and see that we can find the perfect within the imperfect.

I am sure that this book will bring you joy as Orlando shares his personal life with you. As you read this, I pray that you will embrace a quiet relationship with our loving God, even within your own messy and noisy life.

Most Reverend John P. Dolan
Auxiliary Bishop, Diocese of San Diego

STOP GOOGLING YOURSELF

Have you ever played the game Brick Breaker? It's one of those games that are usually preloaded on digital devices. If you're older than thirty, you may remember the Atari version called Breakout.

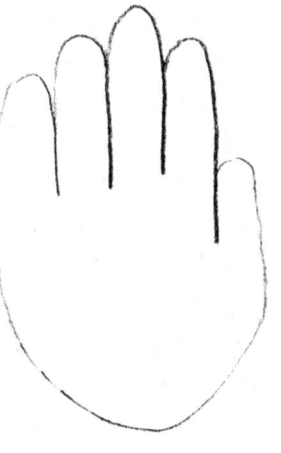

It's a simple game that requires very little skill. It is similar to the game of racquetball. You have a paddle that goes from left to right, and you bounce a ball toward layers of bricks. When you hit a brick, it disappears. After you hit all the bricks in the stage, you advance to the next level. Every once in a while, hitting a brick will release a bonus—an extra life or a laser or machine gun. The funny thing is, I noticed that every time I would chase after the bonuses, I would die soon after.

At first, I was just moving left to right trying to hit one ball. In my attempt to get ahead, I had to hit one ball, catch the bonus, go after the original ball, and press a button to shoot the weapon. A simple game just got complicated.

When I was just focusing on the one ball, I would be fine. It was in the pursuit of the bonuses that distracted me and lead to my death.

Life is pretty similar to the game of Brick Breaker. It starts off pretty simple then gets more complicated when we start chasing after all the other extras of life. Most of our original dreams are to get a good job, find a mate, buy a home, have some kids, and live happily ever after. The focus of most Americans today is buying a bigger house, nicer cars, and sending their kids to expensive colleges. In the chase for the bonuses in life, we spend less time with our family and more time at work. We try so hard to get ahead and actually find ourselves falling behind.

I once traveled that same road myself. Trying to get ahead, I would work an eight-hour shift at the office then work another four hours at home. I would only take a break to eat dinner with my family then back to my home office to grind some more.

The workload never seemed to go down even with all the hours I worked. My to-do list was so extensive that I would actually dread vacations because I feared that it would interfere with my work. In my attempts to overcome the worry, I would actually bring work on vacation. I would leave my cell phone on so that my clients could contact me, and I would continue the grind while everyone was sleeping.

It's comical really; we live in world filled with e-mail, smart phones, and remote desktops. With all this great technology, one would think life would be a lot simpler. Instead, we are so connected that it's actually difficult to separate work life from home life. The tools that were meant to make life easier actually made life more complex, and a great deal noisier.

The inspiration to write this book was birthed on a Disneyworld trip in 2010 where the noises in my life were very evident.

My family and I had finally taken a much-needed vacation. We were at the happiest place on earth, and I found a way to ruin it by focusing on the bonuses of life instead of on my family. Instead of centering my attention on them, I was fixated on the many business ventures I just started. I was constantly checking my phone and googling myself in the hotel.

What does it mean to Google yourself? To Google yourself is to search one's name on the internet in order to see their relevance in the world. You see, in 2009, I had just launched my own bookkeeping firm, and in 2010, I published my first book. With the two endeavors under my belt, I wanted to see if I was significant in the World Wide Web.

This made my wife pretty mad. She was irritated because I was seeking my relevance from the outside world. She was annoyed, and she made sure I was aware of it. At first, I was frustrated for being called out. I tried to justify my actions, but it was a lost cause because I had made promises in the past to put my work aside.

I apologized and said I would improve. So huffing and puffing like a child, I unplugged from my digital devices. I turned off my cell phone and laptop and focused my attention on my family. The rest of the vacation was better, and I have since learned how to leave work behind.

Do you know what the noises of your life are? If you are a stay-at-home mom, it may be keeping the house in order or driving the kids to all their activities. If you are teen, it may be your cell phone, social media, or video games. If you love watching or playing sports, that may be what hinders you.

Some noises are louder than others, like an addiction to substances or pornography, while others may not be as loud but inappropriate in certain scenarios.

Take a look at a drum beat. If and when it is played within the context of a parade or concert, it is regarded as music. However, when it is played while someone is sleeping, the beating of a drum is without a doubt, noise.

The purpose of this book is to share the noises in my life that prevented me from being the best husband to my wife, the best father to my children, and a faithful follower of Jesus Christ. I share the noises that prevented me from living a life beyond ordinary. It is my hope that through my adventures, you may recognize the distractions in your own life. It is my prayer that you discover a way to lower the volume, unplug from the distractions of this world, and listen to the still small voice of God.

Because we live in such a time-sensitive environment, this book is comprised of short chewable stories that you can read in five to ten minutes. After each story, there is a moment of reflection so that you can meditate on what you have read. I hope you enjoy this book for what it is—a simple man's journey of faith.

REFLECTION

Are you living a life beyond ordinary, or are you just existing ("same thing, different day" mentality)?

What are the noises in your life that are preventing you from living an extraordinary life? What can you unplug from today to start enjoying a little bit of peace?

VERSE TO PONDER

Put off the old man that belongs to your former manner of life and is corrupt through deceitful lusts, and be renewed in the spirit of your minds, and put on the new man, created after the likeness of God in true righteousness and holiness. (Eph. 4:22–24)

PRAYER

Dear God, open my eyes that I may see you. Open my ears that I may hear you. And open my heart that I may receive you. In Jesus' name, amen!

FAITH IS A VERB

One morning, my little angel, Jennilyn, was standing in front of the kitchen sink, washing her hands and neglecting to use soap. I asked her to please use soap to wash her hands, and she replied, "I don't have any." I pondered that response from her and mentioned that the soap was right there, just arm's length away.

She continued to wash her hands without soap, and so I again inquired why. She responded, "I don't have any."

I came to the realization that she was never going to move toward the soap. She needed her daddy to give it to her. So I gave in and put some soap in my little girl's hand.

This father-daughter moment made me think. It made me think about how lazy we can be sometimes. Not just my daughter but also myself as well. Sometimes in our laziness, we forget to move. We dream, we desire, we strive for this mythical greatness not realizing it is just within our reach. We just need to move.

I believe we are disconnected from this greatness because we look at things like marriage, parenthood, and faith as nouns instead of verbs. Although the dictionary describes these words as nouns, I believe you have to make them verbs to move them from ordinary to extraordinary.

In a marriage, it's important to come up with new content to feed the conversations with the one you gave your heart to. It's not uncommon to hear of the couple splitting up after thirty years because they have nothing in common. After focusing all their energies on their careers, they find out their spouses have become strangers living under the same roof. If you are not filling your mind with interesting or useful material, conversations become dull, and you may find yourself staring at one another without anything to share. And then the thought appears, "Why are we still together?"

In parenthood, you need to give more of your time to your children because to a child, love is spelled t-i-m-e. Even though they might not say it, they crave the relationship with their parents. If you deny your children your time and attention, they will hold back time from you and eventually their own children. Remember what you do today will be magnified in their lives.

In faith, we look at church attendance as the key to spirituality. But really, church is only a building if one does not move in faith. The Bible is so clear in this.

> *Ask, seek, and knock and the door will be opened. (Matt. 7:7)*
>
> *Forgive and you will be forgiven. (Matt. 6:12)*
>
> *Look I stand at the door knocking if you let me in, I will dine with you. (Rev. 3:20)*
>
> *Faith requires movement, "Draw near to God and he will draw near to you." (James 4:8)*

You see, we need to take action. We need to turn marriage, parenthood, and faith into verbs; otherwise, all we have is a person, place, or thing.

REFLECTION

"Our world changes when our habits change" (Matthew Kelly).

In order to move our faith from ordinary to extraordinary, we have to change our habits, especially how we live out our faith.

Begin your journey by writing down what you want to get out of this book. Habakkuk 2:2 says, *"Write the vision; make it plain upon tablets, so he may run who reads it."*

When you don't feel like continuing the journey, come back to this page to remind yourself why you started.

I CAN TOUCH MY TOES

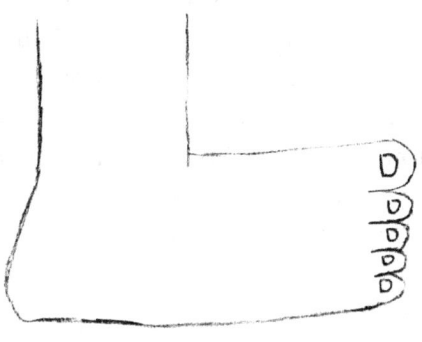

I want share some exciting news! I can touch my toes!

"So what's the big deal?" you may be asking yourself. Well, if you are advancing in years like me, then I'm sure you too appreciate the simple things in life like being able to tie your own shoes, carrying your kids to their bedroom, and being able to touch your toes.

For many years, my mentality was that the bigger the muscle, the better. At one point in my life, I actually dreamt of being Mr. Olympia, the highest prize in the bodybuilding world, and I spent many hours in the gym trying to chase that dream.

After years of training, I found myself unable to do the simple things like playing with my kids, scratching my back, and touching my toes. With all the lower-back pain attributed to excess weight training, I wondered if all along I was building the wrong muscles.

I mean the bigger muscles looked good, which made me feel good, but in hindsight, I see that the muscles weren't any good beyond its looks.

I come writing this story because I wonder if we sometimes build up our worldly muscles and forget to stretch. I wonder if sometimes we spend so much time building up our financial muscles that we lose the flexibility to watch our children grow up and enjoy conversations with our spouses. I wonder if we sometimes focus on building up our ego muscles that we lack the flexibility to ask God for help. I wonder if all our earthly muscles make it harder to move in faith and touch God.

So do I think one should neglect earthly muscles altogether? No. We need to chase our dreams and reach for new heights. I believe we just need to remember to stretch and remain flexible.

I know I need to be flexible to turn off my cell phone and power off my laptop to play with my kids and talk with my wife. I need to be flexible to fall to my knees and ask God for forgiveness and ask for His help. I need to be flexible so I can move in faith and touch the Almighty Father because this life is only but a whisper, and "The grass withers and the flowers fade; but the word of our God will stand for ever" (Isa. 40:8).

REFLECTION

What muscles have you been building? Are you building worldly wealth, a cross fit body, or an ego that you can slice with a knife? How have these muscles helped you?

How have these muscles hindered you in your relationships at home and with God?

VERSE TO PONDER

So I became great and surpassed all who were before me in Jerusalem; also my wisdom remained with me. And whatever my eyes desired I did not keep from them; I kept my heart from no pleasure, for my heart found pleasure in all my toil, and this was my reward for all my toil. Then I considered all that my hands had done and the toil I had spent in doing it, and behold, all was vanity and a striving after wind, and there was nothing to be gained under the sun. (Eccles. 2:9–11)

PRAYER

Not that I have already obtained this or am already perfect; but I press on to make it my own because Christ Jesus has made me his own. (Phil. 3:12)

I press on toward the goal for the prize of the upward call of God in Christ Jesus. (Phil. 3:14)

Amen!

DADDY, HOW SHOULD I PRAY?

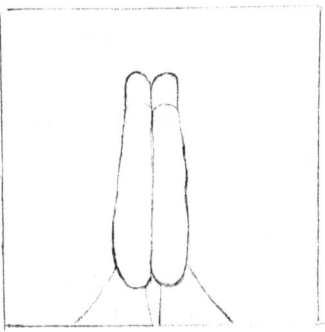

One day, I was in my home office, working. Overwhelmed with the workload I had in front of me, I fell to my knees to pray. As I was praying, my little girl walked in and asked, "Daddy, why are you praying? Is it because you have too much work? Do you want me to pray that you have less work?"

Her innocent curiosity took the stress off my shoulders. Her presence put a smile on my face, and I quickly responded to her question by saying, "Honey, don't pray that I have less work but that God gives me the grace to handle what He has given me."

Prayer is so powerful! I asked for help with my stress, and God sent me an angel to comfort me. Although very powerful, many people admit that they don't know how to pray. If you fall in this category, don't beat yourself up. Even Jesus' followers weren't exactly sure how to pray. In Luke 11:1, his disciples asked, "Lord, teach us to pray, as John taught his disciples."

And in Matthew 6:9–13, he said to them,

> Pray then like this:
> Our Father who art in heaven,

Hallowed be thy name.
Thy kingdom come.
Thy will be done
On earth as it is in heaven.
Give us this day our daily bread;
And forgive us our trespasses
As we forgive those who trespass against us;
And lead us not into temptation,
But deliver us from evil.

Many people know the Lord's Prayer. Many even recite it every Sunday, but how many truly live it out daily? I believe the problem is that many recite the prayer not realizing that it isn't the only way we should pray. Jesus didn't say, "Pray this." He says, "Pray like this." If we want our relationship with God to grow, we eventually have to use our own words. Just imagine having the same conversation every day with a friend or spouse. Now think how intimate would that relationship be?

The rest of the book is comprised of short anecdotes of how I've come to live out the Lord's Prayer in my life. After reading, each chapter come back to the words Jesus taught us and see if it begins to come to life.

REFLECTION

How do you pray? For the longest time, I had the same canned prayer I had since I was a child. "Dear God, bless my mom, dad, brothers, sister, cousins, uncles, aunts, grandmas and grandpas, and all my friends. And forgive me of my sins." As I grew older, all I did was add my wife and kids.

My prayer life changed the day I gave my life to God on August 14, 2007. I now regularly ask Him to reveal himself to me and show me where I need to change. Since then, my prayers have become more like conversations with a friend.

VERSE TO PONDER

"Call to me and I will answer you, and will tell you great and hidden things which you have not known" (Jer. 33:3).

PRAYER

Dear God, I long to know you in the most intimate ways.

"Hear, O Lord, when I cry aloud, be gracious to me and answer me! You have said, "Seek my face." My heart says to you, "Your face Lord, I do seek." Hide not your face from me. (Ps. 27:7–9) In Jesus' name, amen!

I CAN'T FIND JESUS!

> *[When Jesus] was twelve years old, they went up according to custom; and when the feast was ended, as they were returning, the boy Jesus stayed behind in Jerusalem. His parents did not know it, but supposing him to be in the company they went a day's journey, and they sought him among their kinsfolk and acquaintances; and when they did not find him, they returned to Jerusalem, seeking him. After three days they found him in the temple, sitting among the teachers, listening to them and asking them question; and all who heard him were amazed at his understanding and his answers. And when they saw him, they were astonished; and his mother said to him, "Son, why have you treated us so? Behold, your father and I have been looking for you anxiously." And he said to them, "How is it that you sought me? Did you not know that I must be in my Father's house?"* (Luke 2:42–49)

Isn't it kind of funny to think at one point in time, the parents of Jesus lost Him? Not sure if you've ever lost someone before, but it can be pretty frightening. I've got two kids, and if I can't find them in my own house, I freak out. I can't imagine how I'd feel if I lost them for three days.

The verse said that they lost Him because they thought He was with their relatives. I wonder if we sometimes lose Jesus because we expect Him to be with our relatives. I wonder if sometimes we think since my family goes to church, then I don't have to. "As long as they have faith, then that's good enough."

Good enough! Is that really what we should be striving for? Michelangelo once said, "The greater danger for most of us is not that our aim is too high and we miss it, but that it is to low and we hit it."

Jesus calls for us to have a relationship with Him. He doesn't call us to have a relationship with Him through another person. Yes, we may find Him through another person, but the relationship after finding Him needs to be direct. I mean my marriage is only as strong as my direct communication with my wife.

In Revelations 3:20, Jesus says, *"Behold, I stand at the door and knock; if any one hears my voice and opens the door, I will come in to him and eat with him, and he with me."*

You see, Jesus wants access to your heart. He wants to eat with you directly. If you've lost Jesus, then remember that church isn't just a Sunday thing. It's an everyday thing. Mary and Joseph were only out of the house one day. Think about how far we distance ourselves from Jesus when we are out of the house six days.

God wants to be with us daily. That is why the prayer is *"Give us this day our daily bread"* (Matt. 6:11). It's not, "Give us this week our weekly bread."

REFLECTION

Have you found Jesus yet? Write out your God moment. If you haven't had one yet, be honest and return a year later to see if things changed.

VERSE TO PONDER

"*I love those who love me, and those who seek me diligently find me.*" (Prov. 8:17)

PRAYER

"*Make me to know your ways, O Lord; teach me your paths. Lead me in your truth, and teach me for you are the God of my salvation; for you I wait all the day long*" (Ps. 25:4–5) In Jesus' name, amen!

CHURCH IS BORING

One day, on my way to daily mass, my son, Junior, said to me, "Dad, I don't want to go to church. It's boring!" At first, I wanted to respond to him harshly, but how can I blame him? For twenty-eight years of my life I believed church was boring too.

I replied to him, "Son, I understand. I used to think church was boring too. What I would like you to realize is I go to daily mass so that I can learn to be a better dad for you and your sister. I go to daily mass so that I can learn to be a better husband for your mom. Don't you want me to be a better son?"

He replied, "Yes, but it's still boring."

I responded, "Son, there are many things you ask me to do that I don't really want to do, but I do them so I can spend time with you. Can you just look at it as time to be with me?"

He agreed but reiterated that church is still boring. I laughed at his honesty.

Is church is really boring? Honestly, sometimes, it can be, but so can football. I'm not saying this as a football hater. I say this as a former football junkie. I used to wake up at 6 a.m. on Sundays prepping for the 10 a.m. kickoff. I'd listen to hours and hours of analysts break down the upcoming games and watch eight football games at one time. I'm even guilty of watching the little football go up and down my phone while in the Lord's house. "Forgive me, Father, for I have sinned!"

In hindsight, I look back at the passion I had for the game and realize I didn't love the game as much as I loved the activities surrounding the game. I loved gambling, fantasy football, and excessive drinking. But the moment I gave up those activities, the game got boring.

I've come to realize that once an addict, always an addict. But now that I love God and choose Him as my addiction, everything surrounding Him becomes a lot more exciting. I was able to walk away from football because I loved the activities surrounding the game more than the actual game. I won't walk away from God if the activities surrounding Him get boring because He is who I love, not the activities surrounding Him.

I now wake up early in the morning on Sundays to get my wife and kids early to church. I now listen to five to ten hours of Bible sermons daily in order to prepare for the upcoming game we call life. I'm even guilty of listening to Bible sermons while my wife is trying to talk to me. "Forgive me, honey, for I have sinned!"

Because of Him, everything around Him becomes more exciting because He fulfills my needs. He overflows my cup, and His house is the one I want to dwell in forever.

If church is boring to you, ask yourself, "Self, do I want the activities around church to change, or do I want my relationship with the creator of the church to change?"

REFLECTION

What do you think of church? Do you run to it or run from it? Why?

VERSE TO PONDER

"The righteous flourish like the palm tree, and grow like a cedar in Lebanon. They are planted in the house of the Lord; they flourish in the courts of our God." (Ps. 92:12–13)

PRAYER

Dear God, open up my heart that your words may be planted upon it. Put in me a desire to dwell in your house forever. In Jesus' name, amen!

LORD, I'LL SHUT UP NOW!

In my journey to faith, I've encountered many who have said, "I can't hear the voice of God," or "God doesn't answer my prayers." Have you ever said this?

I've come to know that God does speak and that God does answer our prayers; we just don't shut up long enough to hear Him.

I've come to find out in my own life that I don't have a problem listening as much as I have a problem shutting up. An aunt of mine once said to me, "How could such a little boy have such a big mouth?" I myself am very guilty of being in conversations with others and responding before they even have a chance of finishing. I know at times I do this with God, and I believe many others do the same.

In a hurry with our busy days, we rattle off our honey-do list to God and run off and then wonder why He didn't do as we prayed. When I've actually shut up and paused in my prayers, I've come to know that God does in fact answer. In His still, small voice sometimes, He says yes. But God also says, "No, I have something better for you." And sometimes, God says, "Wait, you aren't ready yet."

Many of us can't hear His voice because as quickly as we issue our commands, we are off running. We don't realize that the reason we are on our knees isn't because it's a comfortable position. We are on our knees because God is king and we are not.

Remember the, Lord's Prayer isn't, "My kingdom come. My will be done, in heaven as it is on earth." The prayer is, "*Thy kingdom come. Thy will be done. On earth as it is in heaven*" (Matt. 6:10).

When we fall to our knees in prayer, we are not to bend His will but to be like Jesus and ask Him to bend our own will. "*My Father, if it be possible, let this chalice pass from me; nevertheless, not as I will, but as you will*" (Matt. 26:39).

If you want to hear the voice of God, make sure to stop and listen to Him after you pray. But most of all, you have to read His book so that you know that the voice speaking in your head is God because throughout the day, I hear two voices, and it is only through reading scripture that I can discern the two voices. One leads to life and the other to death.

REFLECTION

Have you ever taken the time to stop and listen to the person you are speaking to? Take the time to just listen. Begin to listen to their heart, not so much their words.

Active listening in the physical world can help you listen in the spiritual world because the word of God speaks to our hearts. If we have trouble listening to someone we can see, how much more will we struggle with someone we can't see.

VERSE TO PONDER

My sheep hear my voice, and I know them, and they follow me; and I give them eternal life, and they shall never perish, and no one shall snatch them out of my hand. My Father, who has given them to me, is greater than all, and no one is able to snatch them out of the Father's hand. I and the Father are one. (John 10:27–30)

PRAYER

Dear God, help me to shut off the noise around me so that I can hear your voice. Holy Spirit, guide me in my Bible readings so that I can discern what I am reading. And please, Lord, grant me the courage to live it out. In Jesus' name, amen!

HEALING BEGINS WITH YOU!

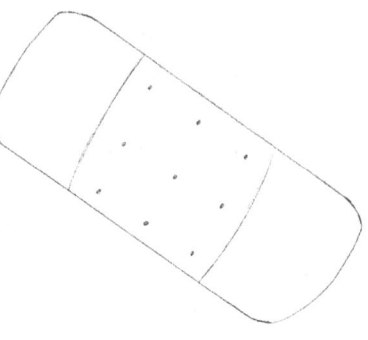

One day, my son Junior got into a little spat with a friend and was heartbroken with the incident. As a father, I tried to fix it because that's what dads do and told him to apologize to his friend. His initial response was that he didn't do anything wrong so he shouldn't apologize.

Note taken; he wasn't at fault, so he shouldn't apologize but I told him that by being the first to apologize, you open the door for healing to begin. He didn't buy it. How could he? He's just a kid.

Forgiveness is one of the most difficult teachings from the Bible. It's difficult for children just as it is with adults. It's challenging for those outside the church just as it is for those inside of the church. I think it's so hard because it seems unfair. Why would anyone want to let someone off the hook for hurting them?

Just as forgiveness is one of the most trying lessons to grasp, it is also one of the most important lessons given to us by God as seen in the Lord's Prayer (Matt. 6:12), *"And forgive us our trespasses as we forgive those who trespass against us."*

You see, forgiveness from God requires us to forgive others. We are measured by how we forgive. Forgiveness opens the door for us to receive the gift of grace, and according to the Bible, *"[God's] grace is sufficient for you, for my power is made perfect in weakness"* (2 Cor. 12:9).

God offers the gift of grace to everyone, but they have to be open to receive it. Imagine a car's gas tank filled with water. Is it going to move? No, because it needs fuel. Now try filling it up with gas. Can you? No, because it is filled with water. Only through emptying it can it receive the fuel needed to move.

God's grace is similar to the fuel as we need to come empty of anger and bitterness to receive his power. Many would think that by forgiving, we are showing our weakness. It is true, but God's grace is made perfect in weakness. When we humble ourselves to others, we invariably show our power in Jesus Christ, the author and finisher of our faith.

When we realize that forgiveness is more for us than for the offending party, then maybe, just maybe, the act of forgiveness will become a lot more simple—not easy, but simple.

REFLECTION

If you are holding back forgiveness, remember wounds won't heal if you keep picking at them. Who are you holding back forgiveness from? Write their names down and begin praying for them. When we learn how to love our enemies, we, in turn, learn how to love those we love even more.

VERSE TO PONDER

Judge not, and you will not be judged; condemn not, and you will not be condemned; forgive, and you will be forgiven; give, and it will be given to you; good measure, pressed down, shaken together, running over, will be put into your lap. For the measure you give will be the measure you get back. (Luke 6:37–38)

PRAYER

Dear Jesus, help me to see how dirty I am in your eyes so that I may see myself not above others. I desire you, Lord. Help me tear down the walls that prevent me from knowing your grace. In Jesus' name, amen!

THE GOSPEL ACCORDING TO FRIENDS

When I was twenty years old, I got a job working for a real estate appraiser, and one of the job assignments I was frequently given was to drive to Los Angeles and photograph commercial buildings. Now for those who don't know me, I want to tell you a little secret: I don't know how to read a map. I still get lost in San Diego; that's why you will usually see me in the passenger seat with my lovely wife driving. I'm a lot better now since the invention of the GPS, Google Maps, and an episode of *Friends*.

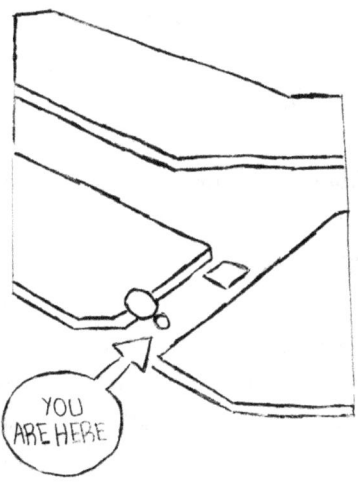

Friends, how did I learn how to read a map from *Friends*? It was the episode when Joey and Chandler were in London for Ross's wedding. Not knowing how to get to their destination, Joey Tribbiani lays his map on the ground and steps on it. In order for Joey to know where he is going, he puts himself in the map. Genius, isn't it? It's just like the maps you find at the mall. In order to get around, you look for the store you want to go to, then you look for the little man with the notation, "You are here."

For those who know how to read a map, this is nothing new, but to a simple-minded man like me, it was pretty profound.

So how does this all tie to the Gospel of Jesus Christ? It too is a simple and yet profound. You have to step into the story. Many have said that the Bible is boring. I've said in the past that the Bible is boring. I've come to realize the reason I believed the Bible was boring was because I didn't know how to read it. Over the years, I've come to a better understanding of the Bible, and if I can give you one piece of advice, try stepping into the story.

In Mark 12:38–44, Jesus tells a parable about the scribes, the wealthy, and a widow.

> And in his teaching, he said, "Beware of the scribes, who like to go about in long robes, and have salutations in the market houses and for a pretense make long prayers. They will receive the greater condemnation." And he sat down opposite the treasury, and watched the multitude putting money into the treasury. Many rich people put in large sums. And a poor widow came, and put in two copper coins, which make a penny. And he called his disciples to him, and said to them, "Truly, I say to you, this poor widow has put in more than all those who are contributing to the treasury. For they all contributed out of their abundance; but she out of her poverty has put in everything she had, her whole living."

Now that you've read the Gospel, try placing yourself into the story and ask yourself, "Am I the scribe who wants to be seen by others? Am I the wealthy who only gives of my excess? Or am I the widow that gives my all?" When I read the Gospel and I place myself in the story, I can see sometimes in my vanity that I am the scribe who wants to be noticed by others, hence the title of the book. Sometimes, I am like the wealthy who only gives of my excess financial treasure. But sometimes, I am the widow when it comes to giving of my time and talent to the church. When I read the Bible with me in it, the stories begin to come to life. It comes to life because I am not reading a stranger's story. I am reading my own personal letter from the Almighty Father. He is showing me that He knows me and can see what's in my heart.

Try reading the Bible in this manner so that when you stand in front of God Almighty and He asks you if you ever read His book, you don't respond, "No, not really, it was boring!"

REFLECTION

Do you know God in the most intimate of ways? Do you want to? If you want a deeper relationship, then read your Bible daily. Father Larry Richards says, "No Bible, no breakfast, No Bible to Bed." Set aside time to read. If you don't set the time, it will never happen.

I like to bring out my journal, my Bible, and a cup of espresso in the morning before everyone wakes up and just sit with God. Don't be so eager to just read the words so you can cross it off your to-do list. The most important thing is not how many times you read the Bible but how many times the Bible lives through you.

Try reading a Proverb a day. There are thirty-one proverbs so you can finish it in a month, and by then, it will become a habit. Remember, "Our world changes when our habits change. Change your habits, change your world" (Matthew Kelly).

VERSE TO PONDER

Blessed is the man who walks not in the counsel of the wicked, nor stands in the way of sinners, nor sits in the seat of scoffers; but his delight is in the law of the Lord, and on his law he meditates day and night. He is like a tree planted by streams of water, that yields its fruit in its season, and its leaf does not wither. In all that he does, he prospers. (Ps. 1:1–3)

PRAYER

Dear God, "Teach me your way, O Lord, that I may walk in your truth; unite my heart to fear your name" (Ps. 86:11). In Jesus' name, amen!

HAPPY WIFE, HAPPY LIFE IS A MYTH

I have some groundbreaking news! I, Orlando Javien Jr., was wrong. To those who know me personally, you are probably thinking, "What's new!"

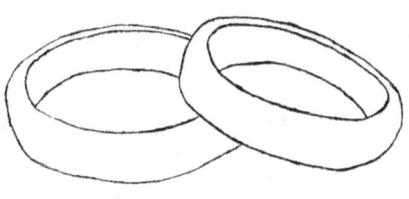

Many a times in my stories and in my conversations, I've always said, "Happy wife, happy life." After further study, I've come to learn that the equation is flawed. It is not flawed in its entirety. It is only flawed in its longevity.

You see, happiness is a result of what happens to you. You can win the lottery today and be happy and have a rock fall on your toe, and very quickly, the happiness is gone.

As a husband, I've tried many times to make my wife happy by buying her stuff. This was easy for me as I knew how to make more money. I believed in the following equation:

If I do something wrong = my wife is unhappy.

If my wife is unhappy = I am unhappy.

If I buy my wife a Louis Vuitton purse = my wife is happy again.

My wife is happy again = I am happy too.

That was the simple equation that went through my mind, and I believe it is among other men. We men are not a complicated species.

The problem with this equation is eventually I had a house full of stuff, and the expectations increased with each new infraction. Now that purse that once filled the void of my wife's unhappiness no longer worked, she now wanted that void to be filled with a diamond or a bigger house.

In my attempts to fill that void, I worked more and spent less time with my family, and the longer away I was from my family, the greater chance for me to find myself in trouble, and the cycle continued.

I've come to learn in my studies that the equation should be—joyful wife = joyful life.

See, unlike happiness, joy is not based upon what happens to you. It is based upon what happens inside of you. A joyful person can lose a job and find blessing in having more time with their family. A joyful person can see their marriage slipping and see an opportunity to lean on God's strength, and a joyful person can lose a loved one and find comfort knowing they are resting in the arms of the Lord. Joy is what we should be striving for.

Okay, so how can one make their wife joyful? First of all, you have to know what joy is. Joy is the second fruit of the Spirit, *"But the fruit of the Spirit is love, joy, peace, patience, kindness, goodness, faithfulness, gentleness and self-control"* (Gal. 5:22).

Now that you know what joy is, you have to know that you can't give to others what you don't possess. If you are without joy, then you cannot plant it upon others.

In order to have joy, you need to walk in the Spirit. In order to walk in the Spirit, you have to allow the Spirit into your life.

How can you allow the Spirit into your life? The first step is to open the door because He's knocking.

Behold, I stand at the door and knock; if any one hears my voice and opens the door, I will come in to him and eat with him, and he with me. *He who conquers, I will grant him to sit with me on my throne, as I myself conquered and sat down with my Father on his throne. He who has an ear, let him hear what the Spirit says to the churches.* (Rev. 3:20–22)

Will you open the door to the Spirit? Will you have a meal with your Lord and listen to what the Spirit says? Or will you say, "This message isn't for me. I can handle it on my own."

The good thing about God is He gives us free will to choose. The bad thing about God is He gives us free will to choose. Will you choose your way, or will you stand up like Joshua and say, *"As for me and my house, we will serve the Lord"* (Josh. 24:15) Because joy follows the man who chooses the Lord and a joyful man = a joyful wife = a joyful life.

REFLECTION

Have you found yourself chasing something that you thought would make you happy, and once getting it, the happiness quickly subsided?

VERSE TO PONDER

"But seek first his kingdom and his righteousness, and all these things shall be yours as well" (Matt. 6:33)

PRAYER

Dear God, help me to seek you more than the things of this world. Allow me to seek after the joy only you can provide. Because this is the day that the Lord has made, I will rejoice and be glad in it. In Jesus' name, amen!

TOO MANY WATER BOTTLES

My wife has always told me that I have too many water bottles. She is totally right, go figure. The last time I checked, I had one in my bathroom, one in my bedroom, a couple on the kitchen counter, three in my office, and a plethora of water bottles on the seats and floor of my car. Some are half-drunk, some are almost full, and some are empty.

The funny thing is, when I have an abundant stock, I will open a new bottle and forget about it somewhere in my house, usually half-full. Then I will get a new one without hesitation.

But when I'm down to my last bottle, I will refill it over and over again until it's so gross that I have to buy a new case.

As I thought about how many water bottles I have, I reflected upon a Bible verse that has always puzzled me. Matthew 5:3 says, "Blessed are the poor in spirit, for theirs is the kingdom of heaven." I couldn't understand why we would want to be poor in spirit. I always assumed we should desire to be full in spirit.

I finally grabbed hold of the verse when I looked at how much I treasured the last water bottle. When I had an abundant stock, I wasted what I had. I didn't maximize each bottle. I used and abused them like they grew on trees. But when I was down to my last one, I began to keep track of it. Even if it was late at night, I would go to my car to get it.

I see that same mentality when everything is going right in my life. When I have an abundance of God's grace, I sometimes forget about Him. I get to this place where I don't think I need to pray as much. My prayers become shorter and shorter, and at times, they become more of routine words instead of an intimate conversion with my Lord and Savior.

Then when I find myself empty again, "poor in spirit," I return to the Holy One with the utmost reverence crying for Him to show Himself again. When I get to that point of humbleness, I am once again filled with His grace.

REFLECTION

The question I ask myself and ask you as well, "Will I wait, will you wait until you are empty, or will you return to God for a regular top off?"

VERSE TO PONDER

"My soul yearns for you in the night, my spirit within me earnestly seeks you" (Isa. 26:9).

PRAYER

Dear God, return to me. Allow me not to be far from you. In Jesus' name, amen

I HATE ANTS!

I am a simple man with very simple pet peeves. I don't like ironing. I despise wet socks, and I hate, no, I loathe ants! I dislike them because every summer, they come into my house with a distinct mission to piss me off.

At first, I just notice one scavenger ant lurking around for food or water. After observing the one and killing it with my finger, a couple of more come out, probably looking for their dead comrade. I smash those three, then all of a sudden, they enter my house like the invasion of Normandy. Troops and troops of ants bombard my house coming out of my sink, cabinets, and windows. If I kill them in the bathrooms, they come out of my closets. When I kill them in the closets, they come into my kitchen. I spray them there, and then they come after my prized possession, my box of Life cereal. "Oh no, they didn't!"

After they hit my holy grail, I hold nothing back and reach for the atomic bomb, I call my exterminator, Earl. Once he nukes my house, all the stress goes away, and no bug will be in sight for months.

One summer, I noticed them starting to creep in. I saw the one and smashed it, and the next day, I saw the three coming in to get their fallen soldier, and I decided to bring in the big guns early. I took preemptive measure and called Earl because an ant attack in San Diego is inevitable. It's not a matter of if they come but when they come.

I made a decision that year that I don't have time to clean up trails of ants, and I don't have the patience to wait for the bug spray to work, and I definitely don't want to find any ants floating in my bowl of cereal.

Okay, I think that's enough ranting about ants. What do ants have anything to do with faith? I believe it has everything to do with faith! You see, sin creeps into our lives just like ants enter our homes. It starts with one little ant, one little sin. Then three more enter our homes, into our hearts, and then all hell breaks loose, and we are overwhelmed with darkness.

The Bible says in 1 Peter 5:8, "Be sober, be watchful. Your adversary the devil prowls around like a roaring lion, seeking someone to devour."

Ants are looking for something to devour, just as the devil is looking for someone to devour. If we don't take preemptive measures in our faith journeys, we can easily be consumed by the things of this world whether it be worldly wealth, the lusts of the flesh, or pride.

How can we take preemptive measures? I believe through regular praying, fasting, and confession. Praying is not a way to call upon the genie of the universe but a way of aligning our ways to God's ways. Fasting is not just a diet but a spiritual act of decreasing while allowing God to increase in our lives. Confession is not a mode of dropping off our trash so you can get some more but a way of emptying our burdens upon the cross and saying to Jesus, "I can't carry this burden. Release me from it, and give me the grace to resist temptation and begin again." It's like David saying to God, "Create in me a clean heart, O God, and put a new and right spirit within me" (Ps. 51:10).

REFLECTION

How will you prepare for your enemy's attack? One of the schemes of the devil is to make us believe he doesn't exist. He wants us to think that he is some mythical creature wearing a red suit and carrying a pitchfork. If we believe there is no enemy, then there is no need for us to fight. Tonight, turn on the evening news, and you will see how real he is.

Just like ants, sin is inevitable. It is not a matter of if but when. Will you call in the big guns early, or will you let your enemy roam around your house eventually consuming not only you but your loved ones as well?

VERSE TO PONDER

The thief comes only to steal and kill and destroy. (John 10:10)

For we are not contending against flesh and blood, but against the principalities, against the powers, against the world rulers of this present darkness, against the spiritual hosts of wickedness in the heavenly places. Therefore, take the whole armor of God, that you may be able to withstand in the evil day, and having done all, to stand. (Eph. 6:12–13)

PRAYER

Dear God, prepare me for the battle that lies ahead. Keep me alert so that the devil cannot take a foothold over my life. Lord, grant me the courage to fight and withstand the schemes of the evil one. In Jesus' name, amen!

MOVE THE COUCH PLEASE!

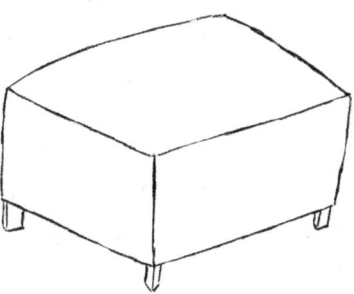

One evening, as I was going up to bed, I noticed that the ottoman was out of place. Instead of it being in the middle of the living room, it was right at the bottom of the stairs. I looked at it and said, "I'll move that tomorrow." I could have easily taken two seconds to move it to the right place, but instead, I brushed the task off for tomorrow.

A few hours later, in a hurry to get my day started, I ran down the stairs and right into the ottoman. After grimacing in pain for a moment, I started to laugh at myself. I was laughing because it was my fault. If I took the time to move the obstacle yesterday, I would have reached my destination more smoothly.

That humbling experience reminds me that I can reach my goals a lot more effortlessly if I only remove the obvious obstacles today. The biggest obstacle that I've faced in my faith journey is an addiction to pornography. It was a vice that began when I was eight years old and continued for over twenty-four years. It was a wickedness that consumed me and almost devoured my marriage. It was only by shining the light of Christ on my sin that the darkness was removed. It is only by shining God's light often that I don't fall back into the abyss.

> *God is light and in him is no darkness at all. If we say we have fellowship with him while we walk in darkness, we lie and do not live according to the truth; but if we walk in the light, as he is in the light, we have fellowship with one another, and the blood of Jesus his Son cleanses us from all sin. If we say we have no sin, we deceive ourselves, and the truth is not in us. If we confess our sins, he is faithful and just, and will forgive our sins and cleanse us from all unrighteousness. If we say we have not sinned, we make him a liar, and his word is not in us.* (1 John 1:5–10)

Many of us have sins that we don't want to share with others because we are afraid of what they will say or what they will think. That is exactly the strategy of the devil. He wants us to stay in the dark and be isolated for that is where we are the most vulnerable. You see, a wolf does not attack the herd of sheep. He attacks the one that wanders away from the flock and the protection of the shepherd.

By sharing, we allow the light to penetrate the darkness, and by sharing, we gain a friend to help us get up when we fall down. By shining the light on the darkness, we can see the obstacles in front of us and arrive at our destination with fewer bruises.

REFLECTIONS

Sun Tzu, a great military leader once said,

If you know the enemy and know yourself, you need not fear the result of a hundred battles. If you know yourself but not the enemy, for every victory gained you will also suffer a defeat. If you know neither the enemy nor yourself, you will succumb in every battle. (*The Art of War*)

What does your enemy look like? Who can you share your struggle with so that the light can begin to shine?

VERSE TO PONDER

Two are better than one, because they have a good reward for their toil. For if they fall, one will lift up his fellow; but woe to him who is alone when he falls and has not another to lift him up. (Eccles. 4:9–10)

PRAYER

Dear God, please help me to reveal my struggles so that I don't remain in the dark. Shine your light, Lord, that I may be set free. In Jesus' name, amen!

THE GOSPEL ACCORDING TO BATMAN

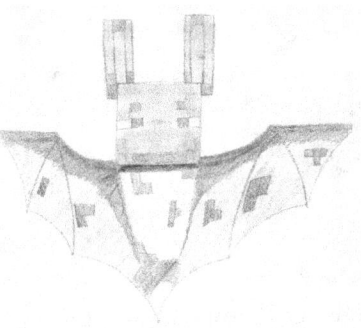

One of my favorite aspects of a growing relationship with Jesus is the ability to see Him everywhere even in the movies I watch. One day, I was watching *Batman Begins* with my son, and one phrase from the movie grabbed hold of me. I believe it empowered me.

These are the words of Rachel to Bruce Wayne after he tells her that he was a good person on the inside. Keep in mind, he says these words as he's leaving a restaurant with two beautiful women, one on each arm. "[Bruce] It isn't what is inside you, it is your actions that define you."

How easy it is to say we are good people on the inside, but in reality, what matters most are the actions we take, for our actions are what truly define what is in our hearts.

The Bible says in Luke 6:43–45,

> *For no good tree bears bad fruit, nor again does a bad tree bear good fruit; for each tree is known by its own fruit. For figs are not gathered from thorns,*

> *nor are grapes picked from a bramble bush. The good man out of the good treasure of his heart produces good, and the evil man out of his evil treasure produces evil; for out of the abundance of the heart his mouth speaks.*

Our words and our actions define us. They define our faith and our beliefs. They tell the world what is growing in our heart. We may use obscene language and say it was a slip up. We may look at inappropriate material and say we fell into sin. We may steal from our employers and say it was a small thing. But the Bible says, "Out of the overflow of his heart his mouth speaks." Out of our overflow, we speak, and as we speak, we also act.

I admit, I am not a perfect man. I struggle. I struggle as a husband, father, and business man. Because I struggle, I ask my Father to examine my heart daily. I ask Him to reveal to me where I need to change. I then ask for strength and guidance to change. Because as a man, I have no power to change others. I only have the ability with God's grace to change myself. But in the act of changing myself, the world around me can also be changed.

REFLECTION

Who have you tried to change in the past? Your husband, wife, kids, friends? Were you successful? Who has tried to change you? Were they successful? Look at your life, and write down one area that needs to be changed and try focusing your energy on yourself, and "Be the change you want to see in the world" (Mahatma Gandhi).

VERSE TO PONDER

Those who are well have no need of a physician, but those who are sick. Go learn what this means, "I desire mercy, and not sacrifices." For I came not to call the righteous, but sinners. (Matt. 9:12–13)

PRAYER

Dear Jesus, help me see where my ways do not align with your ways, and "create in me a clean heart, O God, and put a new and right spirit within me" (Ps. 51:10). In Jesus' name, amen!

DISCIPLINE: PLEASE, SIR, CAN I HAVE SOME MORE!

Mahatma Gandhi was known to have read from the New Testament regularly. When he was asked why he didn't become a Christian, he responded by saying, "If I ever met one, I would become one."

Every day, I encounter men and women who say they are a Christian, yet their words and their actions say otherwise. As I study and walk with the Lord, I've come to the realization that the problem is many may be aiming too low. Many people are Christian by name only. In other words, they only talk the talk and don't necessarily walk the walk.

Now in my study of the Bible, I have yet to see where we are called to be Christians. What I see in the Bible is that we are called to be disciples of Jesus Christ, and we are to make more disciples of Jesus Christ.

> *Go therefore and make disciples of all nations, baptizing them in the name of the Father and of*

> the Son and of the Holy Spirit, teaching them to observe all that I have commanded you; and behold, I am with you always, to the close of the age. (Matt. 28:19–20)

If you look at the root word of *disciple*, you find the word *discipline*, and throughout the Bible, it explains the importance of having it.

> *Whoever loves discipline loves knowledge, but he who hates reproof is stupid.* (Prov. 12:1)

> *He dies for lack of discipline, and because of his great folly he is lost.* (Prov. 5:23)

> *For the commandment is a lamp and the teaching a light, and the reproofs of discipline are the way of life.* (Prov. 6:23)

The Bible calls us to be disciplined, yet many want to wear the name "Christian" while neglecting the discipline part. To wear the Christian name, we have to be disciplined; otherwise, it's just a title. It's like a lady who walks into a jewelry store and wants to buy a crucifix. When shown the different options, she inquires, "Do you have any without the little man on it?" We can laugh, but the reality is, the crucifix without Jesus is just a cross, and the name Christian without discipline is just a name.

In the past eight years of walking with God, I've come to learn where disciplines are needed in my life. I know I struggle with my eyes, so four years ago, I eliminated cable from my home and put filters on all my devices. I know I battle with gambling, so I don't watch football or go to casinos. Overeating and alcohol consumption can be a problem in my life too, so I regularly fast from meat, sweets, and alcohol.

By placing disciplines in my life doesn't mean I'm perfect. I still fall down. But by having them in my life, they allow me to get back up and begin again. Should I trip, I don't have to start at square one; I just have to continue the journey where I stumbled.

If I live a more disciplined life and truly act as Jesus wanted me to act, then I believe others too would like to encounter the Jesus I know.

So to discipline, I say, "Please, sir, can I have some more!"

REFLECTION

Discipline is a form of suffering, but when we know why we must suffer, we can endure. Write down the disciplines that you will put into practice. Start small so that you don't easily give up, and when you fall, just get back up again.

WORDS TO PONDER

I would rather see a sermon than to hear one any day; I would rather one should walk with me than merely tell the way. The eye's a better pupil and more willing than the ear; Fine council may be confusing, but example's always clear. For I might misunderstand you and the high advice you give, but there's no misunderstanding of how you act and how you live. (Edgar A. Guest, *Sermons We See*, 1881)

PRAYER

Dear Jesus, help me to seek out discipline. Allow me to be a bright and shining light that others may want to know you. In Jesus' name, amen!

I DON'T WANT TO DO THE DISHES!

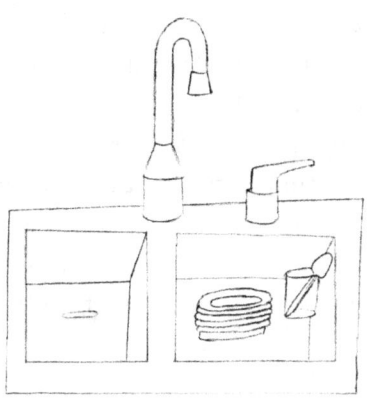

One evening, after a full day at work, I came home and found myself a bit irritated. I got home, sat my butt on my La-Z-Boy chair and began to relax. All the while, my sweet and beautiful wife was trying to get the kids fed and prepare food for a picnic with our friends.

It was only but five minutes into my relaxation when my wife asked me to do the dishes. Now I'm not against helping out around the house, but we had a deal, my wife and I. I was to focus my attention on bringing home the bacon, and she would focus on keeping up with the house.

Now the guys reading this are probably saying, "Yeah, that's what I'm saying!" The women are probably saying, "Oh no, you didn't!"

I then made a comment that irked my wife, and I quickly found myself in the dog house. Though I knew I was in trouble, the dishes weren't done because we were off to the picnic.

We got home late that night, and I again encountered the unsightly scene of dishes overflowing the sink. I looked at them and said, "No, I'm not doing the dishes today. It's her turn!"

I went to bed and awoke bright and early. As I lay there in bed, I thought of how I could avoid the dishes. Maybe I could oversleep so she would see the dishes first, or maybe I could get dressed real fast and leave for work early.

Then after a bit of an internal struggle, God spoke to me through John 13:12–17. In this verse, Jesus humbles himself and washes the feet of His disciples.

When he had washed their feet, and taken his garments, and resumed his place, he said to them. "Do you know what I have done to you? You call me Teacher and Lord; and you are right, for so I am. If I then, your Lord and Teacher, have washed your feet, you also ought to wash one another's feet. For I have given you an example, that you also should do as I have done to you. Truly, truly, I say to you, a servant is not greater than his master; nor is he who is sent greater than he who sent him. If you know these things, blessed are you if you do them.

As the verse began to sink into my heart, I realized what I had to do, and I remembered what I had told another married man. "There is no fifty-fifty in marriage."

"There is only 100/0" (Darren Hardy). If you learn to give 100 percent effort with zero expectation, then you will truly understand how to make marriage work and understand the heart of Jesus. Total and absolute giving of oneself to another.

To that I say, dishes! Bring 'em on!

REFLECTION

Have you ever held back on giving at work or in a relationship because you thought it wasn't fair to give more? What benefit did you receive from holding back?

VERSE TO PONDER

"This is my commandment, that you love one another as I have loved you. Greater love has no man than this, that a man lay down his life for his friends" (John 15:12–13).

PRAYER

Dear Lord, please help me to turn from my selfish attitude so that I can love like you. In Jesus' name, amen!

GOD IS NOT SENDING ME TO AFRICA!

The Great Commission given by Jesus in Matthew 28:19–20 says that we are to

> *Go therefore and make disciples of all nations, baptizing them in the name of the Father and the Son and of the Holy Spirit, teaching them to observe all that I have commanded you; and behold I am with you always, to close of the age.*

In the very beginning of my faith journey after hearing the verse, I pondered the idea that God may send me to a third-world country to preach the Gospel. It was a common story I heard on the radio, a man coming to faith and receiving a call to another world.

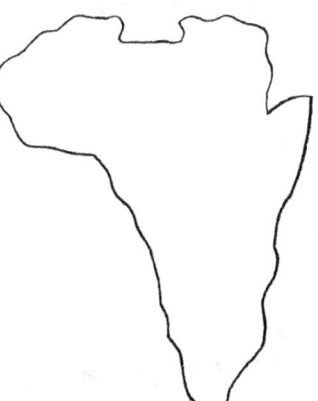

I applaud those men with the courage to uproot their families and leave everything behind for the cause of Christ. But I've come to realize that God won't send everyone.

In Matthew Kelly's book, *The Four Signs of a Dynamic Catholic* his research revealed that only 7 percent of Catholics are fully engaged in their faith. With these numbers, it is clear that there are enough lost in our own backyards.

With much prayer and observation, I've come to learn where God wants me to be. While attending weekly mass, I noticed the confused and unengaged individuals sitting in the pews next to me. I've come to realize that this is my mission field.

I teach eighth grade religious education and have found that not all of my students practice their faith at home. I've come to the conclusion that this is my mission field. As a bookkeeper I have the pleasure of working with many small business owners who entrust me with their finances and occasionally with their faith struggles. I've come to see that this is my mission field. I am a husband and father of two and have come to know that this is my most important mission field.

When one thinks too hard, the many nations Jesus asks us to reach can seem far away, so far that one never does anything with the truth. But if we shut off the part of the brain that controls our mouth and just listen to God's heart, the many nations God wants us to reach is just around the corner, the people we encounter on a daily basis.

REFLECTION

Do you know what your mission field is? Examine your surroundings and see where you can be a positive influence.

VERSE TO PONDER

"The harvest is plentiful, but the laborers are few; pray therefore the Lord of the harvest to send out laborers into his harvest" (Matt. 9:37)

PRAYER

Dear God, open my eyes so I can see where I can be of service. Give me the boldness to step out of my comfort zone to share the love you have shown me. In Jesus' name, amen!

I'M NOT CALLED TO SAVE LIVES

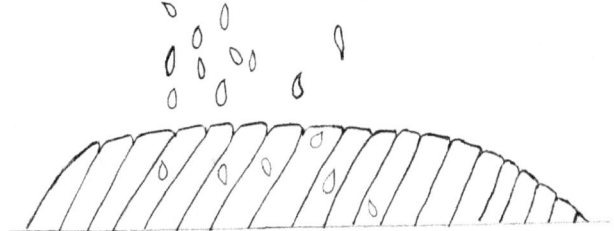

To this date, my journey with Christ has been over eight years. In my walk, God has asked me to do some small tasks like pick up trash and put away shopping carts.

He has later asked me to do much larger tasks like pray for complete strangers, share my testimony to a crowd, and then open up my dirty laundry in my book *God Made Me Pick Up Underwear, Finding Faith In Unusual Places*.

With all the above activities under my belt, one may assume that I've turned many to Christ. To my knowledge, I'm not really sure how many have actually changed due to my activities.

In the beginning, I desired to see many lives transformed right before my eyes, especially the lives of my family and friends. I wanted to see a revival because of my handiwork. To my dismay, I found myself very frustrated when I could not see the fruit of my labor.

After much prayer and counsel from other men of God, I have come to realize that my job is not to save souls but to sow seed. The seeds that I now sow are my witness of a changed life—my smiles, my hellos, and my prayers for others.

Jesus Christ saves; that is why He is called the Savior. I'm only called to be a humble farmer sowing seeds of faith as it is said in Mark 4:26–27,

> The kingdom of God is as if a man should scatter seed upon the ground, and should sleep and rise night and day, and the seed should sprout and grow, he knows not how.

REFLECTION

It's probably a good thing that I didn't see lives transformed right in front of me. If I did, I may believe that I deserved the glory. God deserves all the credit. I am just His hands and feet and a beacon of His light. What kind of seeds will you drop along your life's path?

VERSE TO PONDER

"I am the vine; you are the branches. He who abides in me, and I in him, he it is that bears much fruit, for apart from me you can do nothing" (John 15:5).

PRAYER

Dear Lord, I know I can do nothing without you. Please fill me with your grace that I may shine your bright light upon others, and allow me to be humble enough to give you all the glory. In Jesus' name, amen!

COME SEE A MAN!

How many times have you thought to invite a friend to church and then found yourself talking yourself out of it because you feel it a bit awkward? "What if they say no? What if they think I'm weird? What if they don't even believe in God?" As all the questions pop in your head, you decide it would be much easier to just not ask.

I wonder if we try too hard to complicate the simple. I wonder if in our attempts to share the Gospel of Jesus Christ, we allow our own minds to complicate it so much that we just never do it. I wonder if we look back at one of the earliest evangelists, we might just learn a thing or two about how to keep the simple, just that—simple.

Let me introduce you to the Samaritan woman, the woman at the well from the Gospel of John chapter 4. She was a woman full of sin. In an encounter with Jesus at the well, He reveals all her sins, and He forgives her and gives her the grace to change.

After she encountered Jesus at the well, do you know what she did next? No, she didn't create a website to share her testimony; no, she didn't create newsletter to spread the word about her newfound faith; and no, she didn't go on tour sharing her message. Not to say all the above things are wrong, but she just kept it simple. All she did was say to her neighbors, "*Come see a man who told me all that I ever did*" (John 4:29).

Many times in my faith journey, I've sat in front of a piece of paper preparing to share my testimony and have found myself writing for hours on end. Then after writing a two-hour message and remembering that I am only allotted forty-five minutes, I end up deleting all the complicated stuff and returning to the simple message of, "Come see a man who told me all that I ever did."

There are many times I encounter others who never share their story because they think they need to make it so complicated. As I write, I can honestly say I've tried to make this book complicated. But I always fall back to the simple formula known as KISS (Keep It Short and Sweet).

Why must we keep it simple? We need to keep things simple because we live in a world that is just too busy. Too busy to read or listen to a drawn-out explanation. Heck, we are so busy these days that a company known as Twitter has created a service that allows you to send a message no longer than 140 characters because that's the most people want to read.

When it comes down to it, I've found the most simple and profound method of sharing the Gospel is to tell them, "Come see a man who touched my heart. Come see a man that healed my heart, and come see a man that filled my heart with His love. Come see a man who told me all that I ever did." And He loved me enough to not leave me that way. Come see a man named Jesus!

REFLECTION

Have you ever tried to witness to someone and found yourself somewhat confused? It is easy to complicate faith especially when using church teachings and doctrines to share. Begin to write out your own story so that you are ready to share with others why you have faith.

VERSE TO PONDER

"Always be prepared to make a defense to anyone who calls you to account for the hope that is in you, yet do it with gentleness and reverence" (1 Pet. 3:15).

PRAYER

Dear God, help me to see clearly what you are doing in my life so that I may be able to share it with others. In Jesus' name, amen!

I SEE YOU!

The fruit of Silence is Prayer.
The fruit of Prayer is Faith.
The fruit of Faith is Love.
The fruit of Love is Service.
The fruit of Service is Peace.

—Mother Teresa

When I was around six years old, my biggest fear and recurring nightmare was that I would be all alone. You see, I was the youngest in the family; therefore, I believed that I would be the last to die. That was what I thought until my younger brother was born.

The fear of being alone is scary, and I have a heart for those who feel this way. One would think because of all the ways we are connected via Facebook, Twitter, texting, and email, no one would feel alone. In my life's journey, I've found the opposite. I encounter many lonely people walking in this world. I can see it in their demeanor. I can see it in their faces, and I can definitely see it in their eyes.

After church one day, I approached an elderly friend to say that I was glad to see her. She looked at me with a smile and said, "You know, I really needed that today!"

As I contemplated on this topic, I found that being alone and being lonely can be two different things.

One can be alone without being lonely, and one can be lonely in a crowded room. Loneliness is, therefore, a state of mind, an emotion brought on by feelings of separation from other human beings. The sense of isolation is very deeply felt by those who are lonely. The Hebrew word translated "desolate" or "lonely" in the Old Testament means "one alone, only; one who is solitary, forsaken, wretched." There is no deeper sadness that ever comes over the mind than the idea that we are alone in the world, that we do not have a friend that no one cares for us, that no one is concerned about anything that might happen to us, that no one would care if we were to die or shed a tear over our grave. (Source http://www.gotquestions.org/loneliness.html)

It is shame that there are many walking lonely, looking for a friend, looking for someone to say, "I see you!" That's why I believe many people post their most intimate details on the Internet for the world to see. It meets a need that many of us could fill if we would open our eyes, open our ears, and open our hearts to those that are hurting.

REFLECTION

The Bible says in Proverbs 18:21–22, *"Death and life are in the power of the tongue, those who love it will eat its fruits."* The Bible says our words have power. We have the ability to breathe life into others with what we choose to say.

Who will you breathe life into today? Write their name down and do it. Call a friend on the phone. Take someone out for coffee. Brighten someone's day today, and you will eat the fruit of peace.

PRAYER

Heavenly Father, allow me to shine your light upon those that I encounter today. Allow me to love like you so that they may know I spent time with you. In Jesus' name, amen!

YOU DON'T KNOW ME!

I want to share with you a story about my cousin Peter. Every time we get together for a family function and he is in our presence, we always reminisce about his famous one-liner, "You don't know me!"

You see, one day, while Peter was driving, someone had the nerve to cut him off. Angry by the audacity of the driver, he did what many others would do in the similar situation. He honked his horn and yelled all kinds of obscenities, thinking he would never see the other driver again. That was until he found himself sitting idle, stuck in traffic. All of a sudden, an angry gentleman banged on his window, wanting Peter to repeat the words to his face. Petrified, Peter rolled down his window only slightly and said, "What, you don't know me!"

In Matthew 7:21–23, I hear that similar phrase come from the mouth of Jesus.

"Not everyone who says to me, Lord, Lord, shall enter the kingdom of heaven, but he who does the will of my Father who is in heaven. On that day many will say to me, 'Lord, Lord, did we not prophesy in your name, and cast out demons in your name, and do many mighty works in your name? And then will I declare to them, 'I never knew you; depart from me, you evildoers.'"

"I never knew you." Those are some pretty strong words to hear from Jesus. Why does he say, "I never knew you"? I believe he said these words because many knew of Him, but many didn't actually know Him. Sounds kind of funny, but imagine walking up to the White House doors and requesting to see the president. Do you think he would come down and talk to you? I don't think so! You see, you might know who the president is, but that doesn't mean he knows you.

A relationship with Jesus Christ is like any other relationship. It takes two to form one, and it requires communication for it to grow.

"Well, I prayed, so I'm all good, right?" "I go to church almost every Sunday. I'm all good, right?" I don't think so. That would be like me saying, "My marriage should work because I gave my wife a list of things to do, or my marriage should work because I come home almost every day."

No, in order for a marriage to work, there requires communication between two people, and communication requires talking and also listening. I think we sometimes talk to Jesus and forget to listen. Or we may hear Him but then we figure, "He's not talking to me."

Let's continue reading Matthew 7:24–27 to hear what Jesus says about listening.

Everyone then who hears these words of mine and does them will be like a wise man who built his house upon the rock; and the rain fell, and the floods came, and the winds blew and beat upon that house, but it did not fall, because it had been founded on the rock. And every one who hears these words of mine and does not do them will be like a foolish man who built his house upon the sand; and the rain fell, and the floods came, and the winds blew and beat against that house, and it fell; and great was the fall of it.

You see, if we are to know Jesus, then we ought to do more than our Sunday obligation or come to Him when we need to issue Him our honey-do list. If we are to have a deep and intimate relationship, we must come to Him and talk with Him and listen to what He says. Remember, listening isn't about just hearing. It is about hearing and doing because faith is not a noun; it is a verb.

By actively fostering a relationship with God the Father, Jesus the son, and the Holy Spirit, one can look forward to hearing not these words, "I never knew you," but the words from Matthew 25:23 "Well done, good and faithful servant; you have been faithful over a little, I will set you over much; enter into the joy of your master."

REFLECTION

How do you see your relationship with God, and what are you doing to foster its growth?

If you don't have a personal relationship with God, then take a moment to look at the picture of Jesus knocking on the door, and if you look closely, you will notice that there is no doorknob on the outside. That's because you still have to let Him in. Begin your relationship today by asking Him to come into your heart and speak to you.

Mother Teresa said,

I always begin my prayer in silence, for it is in the silence of the heart that God speaks. God is the friend of silence—we need to listen to God because it's not what we say but what he says to us and through us that matters.

VERSE TO PONDER

"*Be still, and know that I am God*" (Ps. 46:10).

PRAYER

Dear God, help me to turn off the noise around me so that I may hear your still, small voice. In Jesus' name, amen!

HOW MANY SATURDAYS DO YOU HAVE LEFT?

In 2014, I attended about four funerals in a span of six months. That's the most I've ever attended in such a short period of time. After attending all these funerals, it's very difficult not to think about how short life really is.

I got to thinking if there are only fifty-two weeks in the year, and I was lucky enough to see eighty, that would mean I only have about 2,080 Saturdays left. When you break it down in that manner, you can understand when God says, *"What is your life? For you are a mist that appears for a little time and then vanishes"* (James 4:14–15).

When I reflect on that number, I wonder, Am I wasting my days, or am I living life to the fullest?

Eight years ago, I probably wouldn't have been able to answer that question positively. But since taking the road less traveled with Christ, I can now say without a doubt I am living a life beyond ordinary.

Every day has been an adventure since I committed my life to God in 2007. They haven't always been easy but, nevertheless, still adventures. They have become so because I've learned to tune out my own voice and allowed His to rule over me. It is through a life of complete surrender that I can see with His eyes instead of mine.

I can now see when my wife and kids are more important than work, TV, or a football game. I can now see a God moment when it crosses my path. And I can now see when I'm being a tool and need God to set me straight.

Through His eyes, I encounter many people living lives of quiet desperation, people who can't find anything exciting about their day. And I wonder what it would take for their eyes and ears to be opened? What would it take for them to choose the road less traveled? The road that leads to life.

"The thief comes only to steal and kill and destroy; [Jesus] came that they may have life, and have it abundantly" (John 10:10).

I wonder, how many Saturdays you have left, and by what road will you travel them? It is my prayer that you take the time to sit in silence and listen to God's still, small voice. I pray that you come see a man who told me all that I ever did and loved me enough to not leave me that way. I pray that you come see a man named Jesus!

REFLECTION

You've reached the end of the book, and I hope you gained some insight on how to lower the noise in your life. One of the greatest lessons I learned on my life's journey is that knowledge is not power. Knowledge is only potential power. The lessons in this book are only as valuable if used. What tools will you apply in your daily life?

Come back to this book time and time again to remind yourself how to keep things simple.

VERSE TO PONDER

"So teach [me] to number [my] days, that [I] may get a heart of wisdom" (Ps. 90:12).

PRAYER

Dear God, thank you for this day. Teach me to enjoy each moment because only you know how long I have. Help me to see you in my every day and rejoice in your presence because this is the day that the Lord has made. I will rejoice and be glad in it. In Jesus' name, amen!

ABOUT THE AUTHOR

Orlando Javien Jr. is a man of many hats. As an entrepreneur, he runs the freelance bookkeeping and tax preparing company, IAMBookkeeper.

By passion he is a high school religious education teacher, usher and greeter at St. Michael's Church in Poway and a member of the St. Michael's Men's group, Knights of Columbus, Benedictus of San Diego, and Cursillo of San Diego.

Orlando is also an inspirational speaker who loves sharing the lessons he learns from his business life, his faith life and his family life.

As a constant learner of business and entrepreneurship, he shares his knowledge as a networking educator with the global organization BNI (Business Network International).

He has also been blessed to share his faith and life stories to local Rotary and Kiwanis chapters, men's church groups and local high schools.

Orlando is also a YouTube and LinkedIn creator. You can connect with him and view his video content here:

https://www.linkedin.com/in/orlandojavien/
https://www.youtube.com/orlandojavien

If you would like to invite Orlando to speak to your church or business organization, you can contact him at ojavien@gmail.com or his booking agent at https://catholicspeakers.com/profiles/orlando-javien-jr

Orlando's Most Popular Talks Include:
"Do you know Him? How to form an intimate relationship with God."
"God leaves breadcrumbs."
"How to find inner peace in a noisy world"
"How to evangelize with a smile."
"A call to battle: Why men and boys love superheroes."

www.ingramcontent.com/pod-product-compliance
Lightning Source LLC
Chambersburg PA
CBHW052211110526
44591CB00012B/2166